D0602405

American Moments

ABDO
Daughters

THE CONSTITUTION

By Alan Pierce

VISIT US AT
WWW.ABDOPUB.COM

Published by ABDO Publishing Company, 4940 Viking Drive, Suite 622, Edina, Minnesota 55435. Copyright © 2005 by Abdo Consulting Group, Inc. International copyrights reserved in all countries. No part of this book may be reproduced in any form without written permission from the publisher. ABDO & Daughters™ is a trademark and logo of ABDO Publishing Company.

Printed in the United States.

Edited by: Melanie A. Howard
Interior Production and Design: Terry Dunham Incorporated
Cover Design: Mighty Media
Photos: Corbis, Library of Congress, North Wind Pictures

Library of Congress Cataloging-in-Publication Data

Pierce, Alan, 1966-
    The Constitution / Alan Pierce.
        p. cm. -- (American moments)
    Includes index.
    ISBN 1-59197-731-2
    1. United States--Politics and government--1783-1789--Juvenile literature. 2. United States.--Constitution--Juvenile literature. 3. Constitutional history--United States--Juvenile literature. I. Title. II. Series.

E303.P53 2004
342.73--dc22
                                                    2004058365

CONTENTS

$10.00

MidAmerica/Band $

11-3-05

Property of Dexter
Middle School Library

ANARCHY AND CONFUSION

George Washington was anxious about the future of the new nation. In the Revolutionary War, he had commanded the army that freed the 13 colonies from British rule. But independence had proven difficult for the colonies, which had become the United States. A national Congress existed, but it had little power. The states and Congress seemed incapable of dealing with the country's troubles.

On November 5, 1786, Washington wrote a letter to his friend James Madison. In the letter, Washington shared his worries about the nation's condition. Washington was alarmed because the 13 states were working against each other. He feared the country might collapse. "We are fast verging to anarchy and confusion!" he wrote.

The situation was indeed grim for the 13 states. At the time Washington wrote his letter, a rebellion was underway in Massachusetts. A Revolutionary War veteran named Daniel Shays was leading a rebellion in western Massachusetts. Farmers were suffering because of hard economic times and high taxes. They had closed down courts that had taken legal action against debtors. Shays's Rebellion had even shut down the state supreme court in Springfield.

The country faced other problems as well. Spain controlled the Louisiana Territory that bordered the Mississippi River. In 1784,

George Washington

James Madison

Spain had barred the United States from using the southern part of the river for trade. In addition, Britain had closed off trade between its colonies in the West Indies and the United States. The U.S. government had no effective way to respond to these actions.

Britain and Spain were not the only threats. Pirates off of the coast of North Africa attacked U.S. ships in the Mediterranean Sea. The pirates captured cargo and took Americans hostage. However, the United States was too poor to ransom the imprisoned Americans.

As these problems plagued the nation, Madison was working on a solution. He and others had asked Congress to call for a convention to improve the government. The group asked that the convention take place in Philadelphia, Pennsylvania.

PHILADELPHIA

Philadelphia had already played an important role in the formation of the country. On September 5, 1774, the First Continental Congress had met in that city. At that time, much of the eastern coast of North America was divided into 13 British colonies. By 1774, many colonists resented British rule. This relationship reached a crisis when Britain closed the port in Boston, Massachusetts. The Continental Congress met in Philadelphia to discuss a response. By October, the Continental Congress called for a boycott of British goods.

But this only caused relations between the colonies and Britain to worsen. In April 1775, fighting broke out between British troops and colonists in Massachusetts. A month later, the Continental Congress appointed Washington to lead the American forces. Despite these developments, the Continental Congress attempted to make peace with Britain. But in August, King George III declared that the colonies were in rebellion. Britain also hired German mercenaries to fight the colonists.

In the summer of 1776, the Second Continental Congress was meeting in the Pennsylvania State House in Philadelphia. A congressional member named Thomas Jefferson wrote a document that officially announced the colonies' independence. Jefferson's Declaration of Independence listed the colonists' complaints against Britain. But the document also proclaimed that everyone

Benjamin Franklin (left), John Adams (center), and Thomas Jefferson discuss a draft of the Declaration of Independence.

possesses rights. Jefferson wrote, "We hold these truths to be self-evident, that all men are created equal, that they are endowed by their Creator with certain unalienable Rights, that among these are Life, Liberty, and the pursuit of Happiness . . ." On July 4, 1776, the Continental Congress approved the Declaration of Independence and sent it to George III.

The Continental Congress made many decisions for the 13 states. But the states still had a considerable amount of power. For example, each state made its own money and raised its own army. To gain more authority, the Continental Congress developed a constitution called the Articles of Confederation. Congress approved the Articles on November 15, 1777, but ratification by the states did not conclude until 1781. Under the Articles, Congress sometimes became known as the Confederation Congress.

The Articles established a government without an executive branch. Instead, only the Confederation Congress served as the central government. The Congress had many responsibilities. It handled relations with other countries and the Native Americans. Other functions under its authority included the powers to regulate money and to resolve border disputes between the states.

Despite these powers, the Confederation Congress was weak. The laws set up by the Articles hindered Congress's ability to be effective. Each state received one vote in Congress. Important decisions required the consent of at least nine states. A unanimous vote by all the states was needed to amend the Articles. In addition, Congress depended on the states for money because only the states could collect taxes. Usually, the states sent Congress far less money than the amount Congress had requested.

REVOLUTIONARY WAR

*George Washington and his troops cross the
Delaware River during the Revolutionary War.*

The Revolutionary War began because of tensions that had been building between Britain and its American colonies for many years. Colonists were angry that the British continued to introduce new taxes on them without allowing the colonists representation in Parliament. They were also upset because the British passed laws forcing them to support a British army in the colonies.

The colonists committed several acts of rebellion against the British, including the Boston Tea Party. Finally, on April 19, 1775, war broke out at Lexington and Concord in Massachusetts.

France, Spain, and the Netherlands had all joined the American colonies in fighting against Britain by 1780. With French aid, the colonists were able to defeat the British. The United States of America gained its independence from Great Britain on September 3, 1783, in the Treaty of Paris. Besides granting independence, the Treaty of Paris also extended the borders of the United States to the Mississippi River.

The states also controlled commerce and foreign trade. This led to conflict among the states. States with good harbors, such as New York, took advantage of their situation. These states imposed taxes on imported goods that other states had to pay. Congress had no authority to mediate the disputes.

The Articles of Confederation were flawed, but the United States experienced some successes under this government. For example, the United States, with French assistance, was able to defeat Britain in the Revolutionary War.

Overall, however, Congress was feeble. This weakness disheartened James Madison, who had served in Congress since 1780. He complained that Congress had little money and could not support the army. While in Congress, he backed a plan that would allow the central government to collect taxes on imports.

Madison was right to be concerned about Congress's weakness. In 1783, soldiers from Pennsylvania were angry about unpaid salaries. They encircled the Pennsylvania State House where Congress was meeting and demanded to be paid. State officials did not order the militia to break up the crowd of soldiers. Eventually, members of Congress were permitted to leave, and they retreated to Princeton, New Jersey. Soon after this embarrassing event, Madison left the Confederation Congress.

In 1784, Madison was elected to the Virginia legislature. Two years later, he urged a meeting to address problems with commerce among the states. The convention was set to take place in Annapolis, Maryland, on September 11, 1786. Although nine states were committed to the Annapolis Convention, only five states sent delegates. They were Delaware, New Jersey, New York, Pennsylvania, and Virginia.

Among the delegates was Alexander Hamilton of New York. Hamilton had been an officer in the Revolutionary War and an aid to Washington. He had also served in Congress from 1782 to 1783. Like Madison, he saw the need for a stronger central government.

Hamilton, Madison, and the other delegates did not discuss commerce in Annapolis because of the meager attendance. Instead, the delegates arrived at a bolder idea. Hamilton prepared a resolution calling for another convention. This proposed convention would treat issues beyond commerce. It would confront the problems of the central government. On September 14, the convention approved Hamilton's resolution and sent it on to Congress.

Alexander Hamilton

AN ASSEMBLY OF DEMIGODS

On February 21, 1787, the Confederation Congress issued a call for a convention. The Congress asked the states to send delegates to Philadelphia by May 14. Once assembled, the delegates would revise the Articles of Confederation. This became known as the Constitutional Convention.

The convention did not begin on May 14 as planned. Seven states needed to be represented before the convention could begin. But by May 14, only the delegates from Pennsylvania and Virginia had arrived. On May 25, the convention had enough representation to begin. The delegates met at the Pennsylvania State House.

Although the convention started late, it was much better attended than the Annapolis Convention. All the states were represented except Rhode Island, which chose not to send delegates. Rhode Island wanted to keep the national government out of its affairs. The other 12 states named 74 delegates, and 55 of them participated in the convention. Family and business commitments prevented some delegates from attending. Others stayed away because they disagreed with the reason for the convention.

Virginia asked George Washington to serve as a delegate. Washington was perhaps the most admired man in the country. His attendance was expected to make the convention more prominent.

Benjamin Franklin

Gouverneur Morris

At first, Washington turned down the offer to go to Philadelphia. He enjoyed supervising Mount Vernon, his plantation in Virginia. However, Shays's Rebellion had convinced Washington to attend. The Congress's failure to deal with the uprising was another example of the national government's weakness.

Besides Washington, many important leaders attended the convention. Madison attended as a delegate for Virginia, and Hamilton joined the New York delegation. Benjamin Franklin of Pennsylvania was the oldest delegate at age 81. He had helped write the Declaration of Independence, and had signed the document. Franklin was accompanied on the Pennsylvania delegation by Gouverneur Morris, who had been a member of the Continental Congress.

Thomas Jefferson

John Adams

John Jay

Although many of the country's greatest leaders attended the convention, some were absent. Jefferson was serving as the U.S. minister to France. Another leader John Adams was representing the United States in Britain. Adams had been a passionate supporter of American independence. He had also written the Massachusetts state constitution.

John Jay of New York also would have been expected to attend the convention. He had served as president of the Continental Congress and believed the country needed a strong central government. However, Jay's support for a powerful government ruffled some people. He was not appointed as a delegate.

Even with Jefferson, Adams, and Jay gone, the delegates represented a remarkable amount of talent and experience. At least 30 of the delegates had helped write state constitutions. More than 40 had served in the Continental or Confederation Congress. Most had held office in state legislators. In a letter to Adams, Jefferson called the delegates "an assembly of demigods."

The Pennsylvania State House is now known as Independence Hall.

THE VIRGINIA PLAN

Jefferson praised the delegates in Philadelphia. However, he disagreed with one decision made by the delegates. Discussions at the convention were conducted in secret. Delegates were not allowed to talk to anyone about what was said in the meeting room. In Paris, France, Jefferson wrote, "I am sorry they began their deliberations by so abominable a precedent as that of tying up the tongues of their members."

The delegates agreed to secrecy mainly because it would allow them to speak their minds. They could propose ideas without worrying about what the public or state legislatures thought. During the convention, hardly any news was disclosed about the talks. However, Madison and a few other delegates took notes, so historians know what happened at the convention.

One of the first decisions made by the delegates was to elect a president to preside over the convention. The delegates elected Washington to occupy the position. He took his place in a chair at the front of the room where he faced the delegates. He thanked the delegates in a short speech. Washington did not stay seated up front for long, though. He returned to the table where the Virginia delegates were grouped.

George Washington did not participate much in the debates over the Constitution during sessions. It is believed, however, that he lent much support to it at social events outside of the hall.

The delegates then began the serious work of improving the government. Madison believed that a strong national government was needed to keep the country together. But many people in the United States were concerned about a strong central government. After all, the states had fought a war to free themselves from a king. Madison was suspicious of power as well. He believed that people tended to act in ways that benefited themselves. People who held power could be expected to act in the same manner. This could be disastrous for the country.

The solution to the problem of selfishness was separation of powers. This idea held that power should be divided among people in government. Separation of powers would prevent one person or group from having all the power.

On May 29, Virginia governor Edmund Randolph presented a plan for consideration. It was called the Virginia Plan, although Madison had developed most of the ideas. The plan did not simply modify the Articles of Confederation. Instead, the plan promised a strong national government that had authority over the states. But the plan also included the concept of separation of powers. The proposed government would have three branches: legislative, executive, and judicial.

According to the Virginia Plan, the legislature would be made up of a bicameral congress. It would have a lower and an upper house. The people would elect members to the lower house. State legislatures would select candidates for the upper house. Members of the lower house would then elect members of the upper house from this group of candidates.

*Edmund Randolph presented the Virginia Plan
as a way to amend the Articles of Confederation.*

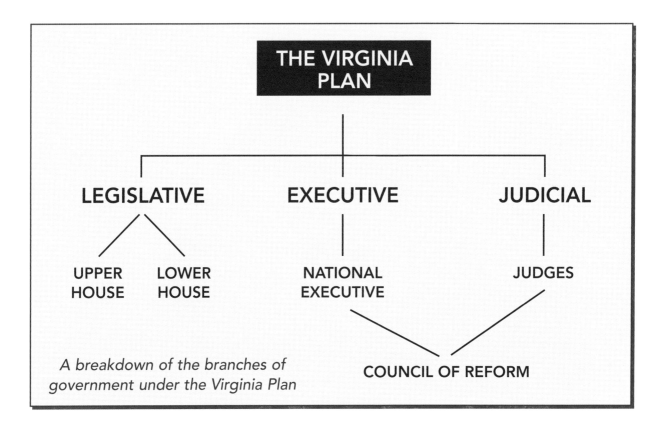

A breakdown of the branches of government under the Virginia Plan

The executive branch would be headed by a position known as the national executive. The number of national executives was not specified. However, this position would be responsible for enforcing the country's national laws. Moreover, Congress would choose the national executive to serve a seven-year term.

Congress would also choose judges to serve in the judicial branch. This branch would consist of one or more courts, which would oversee legal cases dealing with a wide range of matters. The judges would serve for life. Some judges, along with the national executive, would form the Council of Revision. This council would have the power to veto laws passed by Congress.

Of all these proposals, the plan for Congress had the largest impact at the convention. This was because the Virginia Plan called for congressional representation to be based on population. The states with the largest population would get the most representation. In fact, the plan would allow Virginia, Pennsylvania, and Massachusetts to control Congress.

Delegates from the smaller states thought the Virginia Plan was unfair. More specifically, they feared the larger states would dominate the smaller ones. Madison countered with his own argument. He asked why Delaware's 59,000 people should have as much power in Congress as Virginia's 700,000 people.

The convention had reached a deadlock. New Jersey delegate William Paterson scorned the Virginia Plan. He said, "I will not only oppose the plan here but on my return home do everything in my power to defeat it there."

In June, Paterson and other delegates began working on their own plan. The finished proposal was known as the New Jersey Plan. This plan gave much of the power to the states. In some ways, the plan looked like the current form of government. Congress was left the same. Each state would have an equal vote. However, the plan definitely called for more than one executive who would be elected by Congress. In addition, state governors would have the authority to remove the executives.

Paterson introduced the New Jersey Plan at the convention on June 15. The delegates debated the plan for three days. They then voted on the Virginia Plan, rather than on the New Jersey Plan. This vote would decide whether or not to accept the Virginia Plan as the foundation for the new government. The states voted 7–3 for the Virginia Plan. Only New York, New Jersey, and Delaware voted against it. The Maryland delegates split their votes, and the delegates from New Hampshire had not arrived yet.

THE CONNECTICUT COMPROMISE

The Virginia and New Jersey plans were not the only ideas submitted at the convention. Connecticut delegate Roger Sherman had proposed a compromise for congressional representation. He suggested that representation in the lower house be based on population. In the upper house, each state would have an equal vote.

On June 11, the delegates voted on each of Sherman's ideas. The vote totals showed there was support for representation in the lower house. However, the proposal to give members of the upper house an equal vote lost by one vote.

The convention took up the issue of representation in the upper house again on July 2. Again, the delegates considered whether members of the upper house would have an equal vote. This time, the delegates came to a tie vote. Afterward, the delegates formed a smaller committee to work out a compromise. Members of the committee returned to Sherman's idea for representation in Congress. Representation in the lower house would be based on population, and each state would get an equal vote in the upper house.

Another serious problem loomed for the committee. The delegates needed to decide whether to include slaves in the population totals. This decision would have a major impact on the political power

Roger Sherman

THREE-FIFTHS RULE

At the time the three-fifths rule was adopted, the United States had a population of 3,929,214. However, there were more than 697,000 black slaves living in the United States. When slaves were included, the U.S. population increased to 4,626,214 people.

between the southern slave states and the northern states that had started to ban slavery. If slaves were counted in the population, then the five slave states would have as much representation in the lower house as the eight northern states.

A decision made by the Confederation Congress guided the committee. Congress had decided to use population to determine the amount of taxes each state would give to the central government. States with higher populations would contribute more money. In this situation, slave states did not want slaves counted as part of the population. However, Congress worked out a compromise. Each slave would be counted as three-fifths of a person. The committee at the Constitutional Convention adopted this idea. For the purpose of representation, each slave would be counted as three-fifths of a person.

The committee presented the compromise to the convention on July 5. The proposals were known as the Great Compromise. It was also called the Connecticut Compromise because Sherman and the other Connecticut delegates supported it. The delegates debated the compromise before voting on July 16. The compromise passed 5–4.

SLAVERY

Africans who have been captured as slaves

Slavery first began in the American colonies in the seventeenth century and grew gradually as an institution. By the 1660s, colonies had begun enacting slave codes. These codes stated that slaves inherited their status from their mothers and could therefore be kept as property. Slaves continued to be imported from Africa and were used as workers on cotton, rice, and tobacco plantations in the South.

The treatment of slaves on plantations was terrible, with beatings and breaking up of families common. However, the slave trade itself was also bad. Slaves who were shipped from Africa to the Americas were packed together on cargo and special slave ships. It is estimated that 15 to 20 percent of slaves on these ships died before ever reaching port.

Slaves were often traded to the American colonies through the port of Boston. The Americas in turn traded items such as furs, tobacco, timber, and indigo to Great Britain. Britain then traded manufactured goods to Africa for slaves, which would be shipped to the colonies. This created what is known as the triangular trade.

"WE THE PEOPLE . . ."

With the Connecticut Compromise approved, the delegates began to work on drafts of the Constitution. By August 6, printed copies of a draft were available to the delegates. But their work was not finished. The delegates continued to debate, and one of the most serious issues was slavery.

At that time, the United States imported people from Africa to work as slaves on plantations in the South. A proposal at the convention to put a tax on slave importation started the debate about slavery. Many delegates from southern states argued that the states should control the slave trade. Congress should have no say in the matter. Yet, Virginia delegate George Mason attacked slavery. About half the delegates were slaveholders. But Mason might have owned more slaves than any of the others. Nevertheless, he said, "Every master of slaves is born a petty tyrant."

The convention referred the issue of the slave trade to a committee, which worked out another compromise. Congress could not address the slave trade until 1808. Importation of slaves would be taxed as long as the tax was low. Also, Congress would have authority over laws that dealt with shipping and commodities. Moreover, these laws would be passed by a majority vote. This part of the agreement favored the northern states, which had a strong shipping industry.

VIRGINIA BILL *of* RIGHTS

DRAWN ORIGINALLY BY GEORGE MASON AND
ADOPTED BY THE CONVENTION OF DELEGATES

June 12, 1776.

A Declaration of Rights made by the Representatives of the good People of Virginia, affembled in full and free Convention; which Rights do pertain to them, and their Pofterity, as the Bafis and Foundation of Government.

I.

That all Men are by Nature equally free and independent, and have certain inherent Rights, of which, when they enter into a State of Society, they cannot, by any Compact, deprive or diveft their Pofterity; namely, the Enjoyment of Life and Liberty, with the Means of acquiring and poffeffing Property, and purfuing and obtaining Happinefs and Safety.

II.

That all Power is vefted in, and confequently derived from, the People; that Magiftrates are their Truftees and Servants, and at all Times amenable to them.

III.

That Government is, or ought to be, inftituted for the common Benefit, Protection, and Security, of the People, Nation, or Community; of all the various Modes and Forms of Government that is beft, which is capable of producing the greateft Degree of Happinefs and Safety, and is moft effectually fecured againft the Danger of Mal-adminiftration; and that, whenever any Government fhall be found inadequate or contrary to thefe Purpofes, a Majority of the Community hath an indubitable, unalienable, and indefeafible Right, to reform, alter, or abolifh it, in fuch Manner as fhall be judged moft conducive to the public Weal.

IV.

That no Man, or Set of Men, are entitled to exclufive or feparate Emoluments or Privileges from the Community, but in Confideration of public Services; which, not being defcendible, neither ought the Offices of Magiftrate, Legiflator, or Judge, to be hereditary.

V.

That the legiflative and executive Powers of the State fhould be feparate and diftinct from the Judicative; and, that the Members of the two firft may be reftrained from Oppreffion, by feeling and participating the Burthens of the People, they fhould, at fixed Periods, be reduced to a private Station, return into that Body from which they were originally taken, and the Vacancies be fupplied by frequent, certain, and regular Elections, in which all, or any Part of the former Members, to be again eligible, or ineligible, as the Laws fhall direct.

The Virginia Bill of Rights

After the compromise concerning the slave trade, Mason brought up another issue. He believed the Constitution should include a bill of rights, which would protect individual liberties. Mason had written such a document for his state in 1776. It was called the Virginia Declaration of Rights. The document listed many rights, including

George Mason

freedom of the press and protection from cruel and unusual punishment. Other states had based their bills of rights on the Virginia document.

Most of the delegates thought that a bill of rights was unnecessary. They contended that many of the states already had a bill of rights. Moreover, some delegates said that a national bill of rights might interfere with state rights. Finally, some Southern delegates were concerned about a national bill of rights. Many of these bills asserted the equality of men, and this was plainly not the case where slavery existed. Mason's idea for a bill of rights failed at the convention.

A draft of the Constitution was turned over to a committee on September 8. This group was called the Committee of Style and Arrangement. Its task was to refine the language of the document. Although five delegates served on the committee, Morris did most of the writing. He was later known as the "penman of the Constitution."

On September 12, the committee presented the Constitution to the entire convention. The document began with a preamble that gave the reasoning for establishing the Constitution. Originally, the preamble included a list of the 13 states. The Committee of Style and Arrangement changed the preamble so that it simply referred to the nation. The preamble begins, "We the People of the United States . . ."

After the preamble, seven articles describe the function and powers of the national government. Congress would be made of two houses called the Senate and the House of Representatives. The executive branch would be led by the president. A Supreme Court and lesser courts would exercise the country's judicial power.

A SUMMARY OF THE ARTICLES OF THE CONSTITUTION

ARTICLE I — Congress and its powers

ARTICLE II — Executive branch and its powers

ARTICLE III — Judicial branch and its powers

ARTICLE IV — The relationship between the federal government and the states

ARTICLE V — The procedure for amending the Constitution

ARTICLE VI — Establishment of the Constitution as the supreme law of the United States

ARTICLE VII — Procedure for ratification of the Constitution

The Constitution worked out by the delegates included Madison's belief in the separation of powers. In the national government, power would be shared by the president, Congress, and the court system. But the Constitution also limited federal power by setting up a system of checks and balances. Each branch would have powers that affected the other branches.

A few examples show how checks and balances work. The president has the power to veto laws passed by Congress. However, Congress can defeat the veto with a two-thirds vote in both houses. Congress also has the authority to impeach the president and to hold a trial to determine whether the president should be removed from office. The president and Congress also act on the judicial branch. The president appoints Supreme Court justices, but with the approval of Congress.

On September 17, the delegates reviewed the Constitution for their final consideration. By this time, 42 delegates were present at the convention. Three delegates refused to sign the document. Mason would not sign because there was no bill of rights. Randolph did not sign even though he had presented the Virginia Plan. He wanted the Constitution to provide more protection for individual freedoms. Elbridge Gerry of Massachusetts also withheld his signature. He feared the Constitution would lead to the establishment of an aristocracy and monarchy.

Washington and 38 other delegates signed the Constitution. For several weeks, the delegates had worked in secrecy to create a Constitution. Now the rest of the country would have a chance to debate the new form of government.

JUSTICE MARSHALL'S ──DECISION──

The Supreme Court's strongest check against Congress and the president is judicial review. This power allows the Supreme Court to rule that legislation and executive decisions are in violation of the Constitution. The Constitution does not mention judicial review. Instead, judicial review issued from a series of court cases.

One of the cases most closely associated with judicial review is Marbury v. Madison. In 1801, President John Adams had appointed William Marbury to serve as a justice of the peace for the District of Columbia. In order to serve as a justice,

John Marshall

Marbury would need a commission from the government. However, the new president, Thomas Jefferson, rejected Marbury's appointment. Jefferson instructed Secretary of State James Madison not to deliver the commission to Marbury. Marbury petitioned the U.S. Supreme Court to order Madison to deliver the commission.

On February 24, 1803, U.S. Supreme Court Justice John Marshall issued the ruling. He wrote that Marbury was entitled to the commission. However, Marshall decided that the Court could not order Madison to deliver it. Congress had passed the Judiciary Act of 1789 that granted the Supreme Court this kind of authority. But Marshall ruled that the act was unconstitutional. The Constitution did not give the Supreme Court this kind of power.

The decision was momentous. Marshall had ruled that the Judiciary Act was void because it was in conflict with the Constitution. Marbury v. Madison helped the Supreme Court become an equal branch to Congress and the president.

STRUGGLES IN THE STATES

Article VII of the Constitution called for the states to hold conventions to ratify the Constitution. The delegates favored conventions because the state legislatures would be excluded from the process. The delegates believed the legislatures would not want to give up power to the national government. Once nine states had approved the Constitution, it would become the supreme law for those states.

Those who supported the Constitution called themselves Federalists. They supported the idea of a strong central government. However, the Federalists knew that the idea of a powerful national government agitated many people. Consequently, they claimed to favor a federal system, which has general and regional levels of government. The Federalists often stressed the roles of the states in the Constitutional government.

Those who objected to the Constitution were known as Anti-Federalists. They feared that a strong federal government would lead to an aristocracy. Instead, the Anti-Federalists preferred a weak central government. In addition, Anti-Federalists criticized the Constitution because it lacked a bill of rights. This was their most popular argument against ratification.

THE ANTI-FEDERALISTS

Besides George Clinton and George Mason, the Anti-Federalists included such important political figures as Patrick Henry (left). Henry had been a fierce patriot during the Revolutionary War and was a former governor of Virginia. After the Constitution was ratified, Anti-Federalists became the Democratic-Republican Party. This party was also known as the Jeffersonian party because it was backed by Thomas Jefferson. The party supported a strict interpretation of the Constitution and states' rights.

Delaware, Pennsylvania, New Jersey, Georgia, and Connecticut ratified the Constitution a few months after the convention. But as part of ratification, some states proposed amendments to protect individual freedoms. Massachusetts ratified the Constitution with the understanding that Congress would quickly adopt a bill of rights.

In New York, the debate over ratification was intense. People in the New York City area tended to support ratification. Those living in the rural areas generally opposed the Constitution. In September 1787, essays written against the Constitution began to appear in newspapers. In addition, New York governor George Clinton was a leading Anti-Federalist.

But the Federalists struck back in New York. Hamilton, Madison, and Jay started to write articles in defense of the Constitution and the federal system of government. The first article was published in the

Property of Dexter
Middle School Library

New York Independent Journal in October 1787. It was the first of 85 that they eventually wrote. However, they did not sign their names to these articles. Instead, the author was listed as Publius. These articles are called *The Federalist*, or the Federalist papers.

The Federalist papers were intended for readers in New York. But the writings appeared in other states. In May 1788, the essays were collected into book form. It is difficult to tell how much influence the Federalist papers had on ratification. However, the Federalist papers are regarded as one of the best explanations of the Constitution.

Meanwhile, other states continued to hold conventions. Maryland and South Carolina ratified the Constitution by fairly wide margins. On June 21, 1788, New Hampshire became the ninth state to ratify the Constitution. For these nine states, the Constitution became the supreme law. The large states Virginia and New York later ratified the Constitution, but the vote remained close in those states. On June 26, 1788, the Virginia convention ratified the Constitution with an 89–79 vote. In July, New York voted 30–27 in favor of ratification.

Elections were held for the new federal government. With a population of 33,000 people, New York served as the nation's temporary capital. On March 4, 1789, the U.S. Congress met for the first time in Federal Hall in New York City. In April, Congress verified the electoral college votes for president. Congress confirmed that George Washington was the country's first president and John Adams its first vice president. The government established by the Constitution was leading the country.

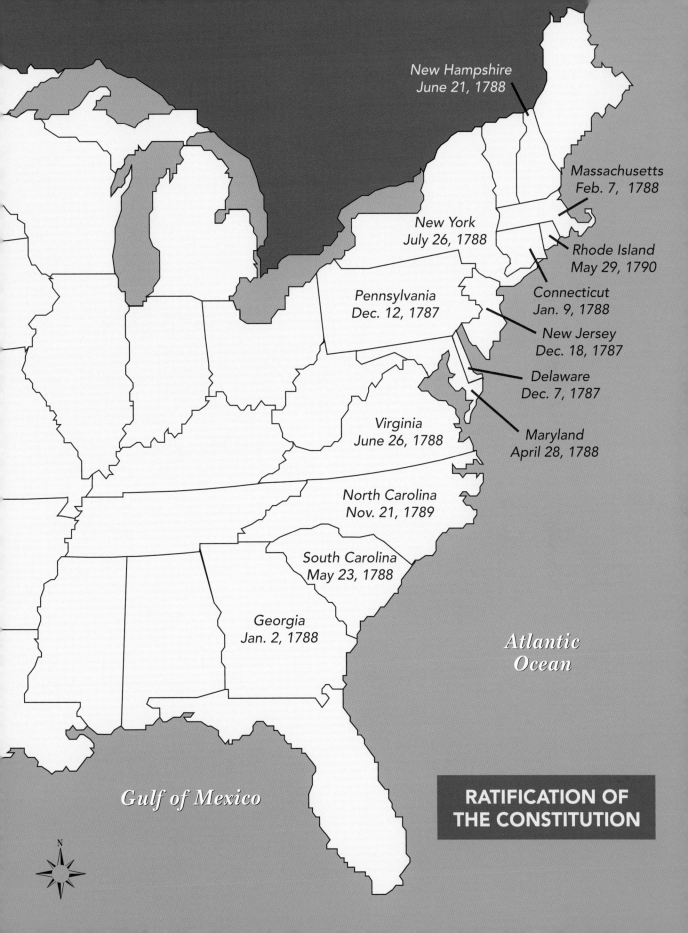

New Hampshire
June 21, 1788

Massachusetts
Feb. 7, 1788

Rhode Island
May 29, 1790

New York
July 26, 1788

Connecticut
Jan. 9, 1788

Pennsylvania
Dec. 12, 1787

New Jersey
Dec. 18, 1787

Delaware
Dec. 7, 1787

Virginia
June 26, 1788

Maryland
April 28, 1788

North Carolina
Nov. 21, 1789

South Carolina
May 23, 1788

Georgia
Jan. 2, 1788

*Atlantic
Ocean*

Gulf of Mexico

**RATIFICATION OF
THE CONSTITUTION**

N

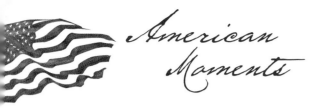

BILL OF RIGHTS

Ratification of the Constitution did not halt discussion of a bill of rights. The states' demand for a bill of rights forced Madison to admit that such a bill was needed. As a newly elected member to the House of Representatives, he began to work on one. He examined amendments proposed during the state conventions. Madison also drew on ideas found in the Virginia Declaration of Rights. By June 1789, Madison presented a bill of rights to Congress.

In Congress, a committee of three senators and three representatives considered Madison's bill. In September, the committee arranged the bill into 12 amendments, which were sent to the states for ratification.

Progress toward a bill of rights helped convince North Carolina and Rhode Island to finally ratify the Constitution. North Carolina approved the Constitution on November 21, 1789. Rhode Island was the final state of the original 13 colonies to ratify the Constitution. But the vote at the state convention had been close. On May 29, 1790, Rhode Island delegates voted 34–32 for ratification.

Meanwhile, the states considered the bill of rights. The states rejected two amendments about the structure and payment of Congress. However, three-fourths of the states ratified the other ten amendments by December 15, 1791. These ten amendments, known as the Bill of Rights, had become part of the Constitution.

AMENDING THE CONSTITUTION

The process to amend the Constitution can begin one of two ways. Congress may propose an amendment by a two-thirds vote in both the Senate and the House of Representatives. States may also begin the amendment process. State legislatures may propose legislation by a vote of two-thirds of the states. A convention may also be called by two-thirds of the states to propose an amendment. Although both Congress and the states may propose legislation, only Congress has ever done so since the Constitutional Convention.

After an amendment has passed the two-thirds vote, it is sent to the states for ratification. For an amendment to be added to the Constitution, three-fourths, or 38 out of 50, of the states must approve it. The states may do this by taking a vote in the state legislature or by calling a convention within the state.

When an amendment passes in the required number of states, the U.S. National Archives and Records Administration's Office of the Federal Register (OFR) certifies the amendment. This certification is then signed by witnesses. Though the president has no official part in the amendment process, many have served as witnesses.

The Bill of Rights

The Bill of Rights proclaims some of the most basic freedoms in the United States. These freedoms recognize the dignity of the individual. They set limits on the government. Some of the most important rights are named in the First Amendment. This amendment protects freedom of religion, speech, assembly, and the press. The amendment also guarantees people the right to petition the government.

The history of the U.S. Constitution continues beyond the Bill of Rights. The Constitution has inspired other nations to enact written constitutions. Poland and France adopted written constitutions in 1791. Since then, many other countries have followed the example of the United States. In the early twenty-first century, most nations have written constitutions.

However, there is at least one major difference between the constitutions of the United States and several other nations. Many countries have rewritten their constitutions. The United States has not. For more than 200 years, the United States has relied on the laws and form of government set forth in the Constitution. It is the oldest written constitution that is still in effect.

The Constitution has endured for so long for several reasons. One reason is that the Constitution established a government that answers to the American people. Americans can influence the government through elections. They directly elect members of Congress and they choose electors who vote for the president. Also, the First Amendment of the Constitution secures individual rights. Under the protection of these rights, the American people can protest against the government.

Another reason the Constitution abides is that it can be amended to reflect changing conditions and views. For example, at the Constitutional Convention, the delegates accepted slavery, even

Visitors to the National Archives Building view the Constitution.

though many of them opposed it. But in 1865, the Thirteenth Amendment abolished slavery. In fact, since 1790 the Constitution has been amended 27 times.

The original U.S. Constitution is on display at the National Archives Building in Washington DC. But the Constitution is not simply a document preserved in a case. The Constitution is called a living document because it continues to affect the lives of Americans. It professes the nation's chief laws and freedoms. United States Supreme Court justice William J. Brennan Jr. praised the enduring importance of the Constitution in 1985. He said, "The genius of the Constitution rests not in any static meaning it might have had in a world that is dead and gone, but in the adaptability of its great principles to cope with current problems and current needs. . . ."

The Constitution, and more specifically the Bill of Rights, gives Americans many rights. Since the ratification of the Constitution and the Bill of Rights, many Americans have exercised their rights to make changes in society and government. As shown here, many African Americans marched with Martin Luther King Jr. in Washington DC in 1963 to protest the unfair treatment of African Americans in society.

These marchers were protected by the First Amendment, which guarantees the "right of the people to peaceably assemble, and to petition the Government for a redress of grievances." King and the marchers hoped to push Congress to pass civil rights legislation protecting the rights of African Americans.

TIMELINE

1774   On September 5, the First Continental Congress meets in Philadelphia, Pennsylvania.

1775   In April, the Revolutionary War begins in Massachusetts.

1776   On July 4, the Second Continental Congress approves the Declaration of Independence.

1777   On November 15, the Second Continental Congress approves the Articles of Confederation. The Articles are ratified in 1781.

1783   The Treaty of Paris ends the Revolutionary War. The United States's borders are extended to the Mississippi River and Britain recognizes U.S. independence.

1786   Farmers suffering economic hardship follow Daniel Shays into Shays's Rebellion. This and other events, such as Spain's blocking of trade on the Mississippi River, cause concern about the weak U.S. government.

On September 11, delegates from five states meet in Annapolis, Maryland, to discuss interstate commerce. Delegates instead arrange a convention to revise the Articles of Confederation.

1787   On May 25, the convention to revise the Articles of Confederation begins.

Edmund Randolph presents the Virginia Plan to the convention on May 29.

On June 15, William Paterson presents the New Jersey Plan to the convention. Three days later, the Virginia Plan becomes the framework for the Constitution.

The Great Compromise, or Connecticut Compromise, is adopted by the convention on July 16.

On September 17, all but three delegates to the Constitutional Convention sign the Constitution. The document is then submitted to the states for ratification.

In October, Alexander Hamilton, James Madison, and John Jay begin publishing the Federalist papers.

1788 On June 21, New Hampshire becomes the ninth and final necessary state to ratify the Constitution.

1789 In June, Madison presents a draft of a bill of rights to Congress. Congress later sends 12 amendments to the states for ratification.

1790 Rhode Island becomes the last state to ratify the Constitution in May.

1791 In December, the ten amendments that became the Bill of Rights are ratified and added to the Constitution.

American Moments

FAST FACTS

Nathaniel Gorham of Massachusetts chaired some of the proceedings at the Constitutional Convention. Delegates did not know, however, that Gorham had written to Prince Henry of Prussia and suggested he become king of the United States.

Charles Pinckney of South Carolina presented a plan for government on the same day the Virginia Plan was revealed. Known as the Pinckney Plan, the original document of the proposal has never been found. This has caused some historical debate about its existence. However, notes from delegates at the Constitutional Convention talk about the plan.

Historians knew that Alexander Hamilton, James Madison, and John Jay had written the Federalist papers. But for a long time, researchers did not know which author had written each of the essays. Computer analysis later helped answer this question. Most historians now believe that Hamilton wrote essays 1, 6–9, 11–13, 15–17, 21–36, 59–61, and 65–85. Jay wrote essays 2–5 and 64. Madison most likely wrote 10, 14, 18–20, 37–58, and 62–63.

Connecticut and Georgia did not ratify the Bill of Rights until 1939, 150 years after the ratification of the Constitution. Both states had believed the amendments unnecessary. Massachusetts also did not officially ratify the Bill of Rights until that year. Both houses of its legislature had accepted most of the amendments by 1790. However, an official ratification notice had never been sent to the U.S. government.

During World War II, the Declaration of Independence and the Constitution were housed at Fort Knox, Kentucky. The documents were transferred to this secure location just two weeks after the bombing of Pearl Harbor on December 7, 1941, for safekeeping.

WEB SITES
WWW.ABDOPUB.COM

Would you like to learn more about the Constitution? Please visit **www.abdopub.com** to find up-to-date Web site links about the Constitution and other American moments. These links are routinely monitored and updated to provide the most current information available.

Delegates to the Constitutional Convention sign the completed Constitution.

GLOSSARY

aristocracy: people who are born into a high social class. These people run the government in some countries.

bicameral: consisting of or having two chambers.

commerce: the buying or selling of goods on a large scale.

demigod: a person so outstanding he or she seems to be almost a god.

dignity: the quality being proud or having self-respect.

economy: the way a nation uses its money, goods, and natural resources.

electoral college: the group that elects the president and vice president by casting electoral votes. When people vote for a president, the political party that gets the most votes in each state sends a representative to the electoral college. There, the representatives vote for their party's candidate.

goods: property other than money that has value.

impeach: to have a trial to see if a person should be removed from office.

legislature: a group organized to make and repeal laws for a state or nation.

mercenary: a soldier hired for money who generally serves in a foreign military.

militia: a group of citizens trained for war or emergencies.

monarchy: a government controlled by a king or queen.

petition: to make a formal request to a person of authority.

preamble: an introduction to a formal document.

precedent: something said or done that sets an example for future actions.

ratify: to officially approve.

static: unchanging.

unalienable: something that cannot be given away or taken away, such as rights.

veto: the right of one member of a decision-making group to stop an action by the group.

INDEX